Hill's™

With the compliments of Hill's Pet Nutrition

D1461273

You and your dog have a special bond which has grown over the years. Your dog really is part of the family, after all, they do say that a dog is "man's best friend". It may come as a surprise to learn that your dog, having reached the age of five is considered to have entered the senior stage of life.

During this stage of life your dog's needs are changing, but much of this change will have gone unnoticed. However, comparing the age of your dog to their 'human age' will help you understand just how important this stage of life can be. Did you know that a five year old large breed dog is considered to be of an equivalent age to a 45 year old person?

*“**The best thing about a man is his dog.***”*

French Proverb

Remember that old age isn't an illness and does not necessarily mean ill health. It is simply that older dogs work differently. This is a time of life when several conditions are more likely to occur and when extra attention should be paid to your dog's needs.

This book will give you simple practical tips on how to best care for your dog and will help you recognise the early signs of ageing. A few small changes now can make a big difference, and by working with your vet you will ensure your dog keeps getting the very most out of life.

" Old age is not an illness and does not necessarily mean ill health. "

Dog Fact

The Irish Wolfhound is the tallest breed of dog in the world

Some older dogs spend more time asleep. Combine this with stiff joints and it is easy to understand why a nice soft padded bed is preferable for your older canine companion.

This might be a good time to think about where your dog actually sleeps. If he has always slept upstairs then try to get him used to being downstairs. Saving a long climb up the stairs at night can be kinder to old joints. Coming up and down stairs can also place additional strain on the back.

If your dog has lost weight with his increasing age, then extra warmth at night time can be valuable. Why not consider a heat pad under his bedding, especially in the winter months!

Older dogs tend to become wobbly on their legs, especially if they have arthritis. You might need to think about the floors they have to walk on. If you have lots of polished wood floors or slippery ceramic tiles in your house, then using a few non-slip rugs can help avoid slips and falls.

Old age may be the start of poor eyesight. Help your dog by keeping the home environment the same, as much as possible. If your dog does have trouble seeing, try not to move furniture around too much – or if you do then guide him round these new obstacles the first few times, until he learns where everything is.

Older dogs tend to get wobbly on their legs especially if they have arthritis.

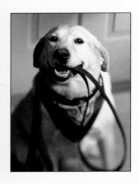

'You can't teach an old dog new tricks'. I'm sure you've heard that said and it is easy to see what is meant by it. Many older dogs seem forgetful or confused. They often lose their normal house training habits and appear short tempered.

These behavioural changes are a common part of the ageing process, but don't accept them as inevitable. New research has shown that there is a lot that can be done to improve the quality of your dog's life and lessen these signs. If you notice your dog gets lost on walks, is restless at night, or doesn't greet you when you return home, he may be starting to show signs of brain ageing.

You can't teach an old dog new tricks?

Dog Fact

The basenji is the only dog that cannot bark

You may notice some or all of the following:

✗ Waking at night

✗ Restlessness

✗ Barking at previously familiar things or people

✗ Loss of house training habits

✗ Fears or phobias

✗ Becoming anxious when left alone

✗ Unusual aggression

If you have noticed these signs then ask your vet to check your dog. It may be that he will benefit from a change of diet or some medication. Special diets and medications are now available that have been shown to significantly improve many of these behaviours.

Older dogs may need to sleep for longer and will appear less able to cope with changes in their routine or surroundings. You need to bear these things in mind when planning any changes in your older dog's routine. Moving home is a stressful time for us, but can be even more difficult for a senior dog. A new baby or puppy are exciting and enjoyable occasions for us, but can be stressful for an older pet.

This doesn't mean that older dogs cannot cope with any change. In fact, a new puppy can be a very welcome addition to the family. By encouraging them to play and interact, the new puppy can be a breath of fresh air to his older companion.

A few simple rules will ease the introduction of a new puppy. Try to match the sizes of the two dogs. Make sure the puppy has a place to go when he wants to rest, or when the older dog needs some time out. It is worth investing in a puppy crate to make sure both dogs can get some peace and quiet when needed.

> **Think about a pet buddy for your best friend.**

The right companion can make a real difference to an older dog. After all, dogs are naturally very sociable and do not like being alone. So if you don't have one, think about a pet buddy for your best friend.

A few small changes now will help your dog keep his bright smile. Although dental problems are by far the most common disorder seen in older dogs, as with many things, prevention is better than cure. We are all used to brushing our teeth twice a day, it's just a normal part of our daily routine. Unfortunately, most pets don't get the same kind of dental care. Just imagine how your mouth would feel if you hadn't brushed your teeth for five years!

Combine this lack of tooth brushing with a soft diet that tends to stick to the teeth and you can easily see why dental problems are so common.

If you spot any of the following signs then it is possible your older dog has dental problems:

✗ Bad breath. Many people think that doggy breath is normal, but if your dog's breath smells bad then it might indicate dental disease and infection

✗ Brown teeth. This may be due to a build up of tartar on the teeth and is most often found on the large teeth at the back of the mouth

✗ Dribbling

✗ Rubbing the face or mouth

✗ Swelling on the face, especially under one eye

✗ Bleeding gums

✗ Poor appetite or trouble eating. Maybe you have noticed your dog always eats on one side

If you spot any of these, ask your vet for a dental check up as your dog may have gum disease. Treatment of gum disease is important because the presence of plaque and tartar in the mouth has been shown to increase the risk of both kidney and heart disorders.

Your vet may suggest professional teeth cleaning, a course of antibiotics and a change of diet. It may be too late to get your older dog to accept daily tooth brushing but anything you can achieve will help to keep his teeth clean and his breath fresh.

Rope toys are a good idea as they act a bit like dental floss.

Don't be worried if your vet does suggest a professional teeth cleaning. Although this is performed under a general anaesthetic, modern medications and techniques are very safe. Your vet may want to take a blood sample before giving the anaesthetic. This checks that your dog's kidneys and liver are working well enough to break the medication down which will ensure the anaesthetic will be well tolerated.

Encouraging your older dog to chew will help to keep his teeth clean. Knotted rope toys are a good idea as they act a bit like dental floss. You can also get special dental toys and rawhide dental chews that work to keep both the teeth and gums healthy.

> **Using a good quality dog shampoo will hydrate the skin**

Just because your dog is getting older doesn't mean he won't still benefit from a regular wash and brush up. Help keep your dog looking his best by daily grooming which will also allow you the chance to both touch and look at your dog each day, which will make problems much easier to spot. Brushing your dog stimulates the skin, improves blood flow and reduces the build up of dead hair and skin. This can make the coat appear much healthier.

Regular shampooing will also benefit your older dog by reducing skin bacteria and therefore lessening any odour. Using a good quality dog shampoo will hydrate the skin, not dry it out, leaving the coat feeling soft and healthy, not dry and flaky. Drying your dog thoroughly is very important, as they will be less tolerant of the cold.

Dog Fact

Every known dog except the Chow has a pink tongue – the Chow's tongue is black

Large breed dogs may develop patches of hard skin called calluses on their elbows or hips. You can prevent these by ensuring your dog always has a soft padded place to rest and discouraging him from lying on hard surfaces. If calluses do form then rubbing a mild hand cream into them will help soften the skin and prevent infection developing.

Many skin and coat problems will respond to simple changes in your dog's diet. Providing a senior food that is rich in essential fatty acids, vitamins and zinc, can be all that is needed to see a significant improvement in the quality and appearance of your dog's coat.

> **Older dogs generally gain weight as they become less active.**

As we get older our dietary needs change. None of us eat the same things as adults as we did when we were babies or teenagers. The same is true for older dogs, but surprisingly lots of people keep feeding their dogs the same food throughout life.

Middle aged dogs generally gain weight as they become less active. Switching to a special senior dog food that contains slightly fewer calories can help your dog maintain their ideal body weight. If your dog does seem to be losing weight then a more digestible, more energy dense food may be needed.

Dog Fact

Chocolate is toxic to dogs

Reduced activity can also lead to constipation. Choosing a food with a slightly higher amount of fibre can ease this condition.

Dogs become more prone to kidney problems as they get older. It has been shown that by controlling the intake of certain nutrients you can slow down the progression of kidney problems.

There is a vast array of different dog foods available today and the choice can be rather confusing. Look out for these things to guide you towards the best diet for your dog:

✓ Controlled phosphorus

✓ Controlled protein

✓ Controlled salt

✓ Moderately increased fibre

✓ Enriched with vitamins and minerals

✓ Good for the teeth

Ask your vet for a recommendation

Older dogs will generally be less tolerant of the attentions of an enthusiastic young child than a small puppy would be. Children also tend to behave in an unpredictable way and this can startle an older dog, especially if they have impaired hearing or sight.

This can lead to a normally placid dog snapping at a child unexpectedly. Avoid this by allowing your dog a safe haven away from small visitors and by teaching your children the right way to behave around animals.

Simple rules such as ensuring the dog is stroked properly and not disturbed whilst sleeping or eating will go a long way to ensuring all the family remain happy.

Dog Fact

33 percent of dog owners admit that they talk to their dogs on the phone

If you are thinking of bringing a new pet into the family then consideration must be given to how your older dog will react. Choose the breed of a new puppy carefully. A very boisterous breed may not be welcomed and even a small kitten can be an annoyance rather than a welcome addition to the household. Your vet may be able to help you to select the best pet.

Do remember that if you introduce a young puppy then you must be prepared to treat your two dogs as individuals. Your older dog will require a different diet and a different exercise regimen to your young pup. Are you ready and able to provide these differences?

Dogs are generally more sociable than cats and prefer the company of other dogs. If you do wish to introduce a new pet then the following tips may ease the transition:

✓ Choose the new pet carefully

✓ Initial introductions should be gradual and supervised

✓ Provide an indoor pen for the new pet

✓ Provide separate feeding areas and beds

✓ Play with both animals as much as possible

✓ Consider using canine pheromones

Exercise is vital. Not only does exercise play an important role in maintaining physical fitness, it is also key to mental stimulation. As they say, a healthy mind means a healthy body. Older dogs that are confined for long periods of the day with little social contact will become depressed and withdraw from their surroundings. Dogs are intensely social creatures. Whilst they may seem to accept humans as pack leaders, our company cannot compensate for the smells and experiences of the local field.

> **Dogs are intensely social creatures.**

Daily exercise is also needed to maintain muscle strength and stamina. This means that regular exercise is very important, especially as your dog gets older. Try not to save all the week's activity and exercise for the great long walks at the weekends. Staggering the exercise over the whole week will result in a fitter, happier dog.

Exercise will also help prevent your dog becoming overweight. If an older dog is allowed to become fat it may never fully regain the ability to exercise.

Other beneficial effects of regular exercise include:

✓ Prevention of constipation

✓ Helps maintain heart function

✓ Keeps muscles toned

✓ Keeps joints moving and so reduces effects of arthritis

It cannot be stressed how important it is to control the rate and frequency of exercise for older dogs. Over enthusiastic or excessively long periods of exercise may cause more problems that it eases. Arthritic dogs may appear to keep going all day, but they can often be stiff and uncomfortable the next morning.

There will be times when you wish to take your older dog out in the car with you. Being aware of a few simple changes can make car journeys more pleasant for your older canine companions. Elderly dogs may not be able to keep their balance in the back of a moving car. Try putting their bed in the back of the car to improve stability.

Remember to never leave your dog unattended in a car when the weather is hot. This is even more vital as your dog gets older, because older dogs are less able to cope with environmental changes. Older dogs are much more susceptible to heat stress and may also be affected by heart and lung conditions that will increase their vulnerability.

Lots of people take their dog on holiday with them and with the Pet Travel Scheme*, we can now even take our dogs throughout Europe. It's not too late to get your dog ready for a holiday. You simply need to follow a few basic steps and then your dog can travel freely between countries.

- ✓ Firstly your dog must be microchipped. A small microchip is implanted under the skin. This chip contains a number that is unique for your dog. The number links your dog to your contact details on a database

- ✓ Your vet will then have to vaccinate your dog against rabies

- ✓ 30 days after the rabies vaccination, your vet will take a blood sample and send it to a special laboratory. Here the sample will be tested to make sure your dog has a good immunity to rabies

- ✓ Once the blood test has been passed, your vet will issue you with a Pets Passport

- ✓ Regular booster vaccinations are needed to maintain your dog's immunity to rabies and to keep your passport up to date

*for more information, see: http://www.defra.gov.uk

If you choose to leave your dog at home then boarding kennels are the usual next port of call. If you have not used a particular kennel before, then do visit and inspect the facilities before leaving your pet there. Make sure the kennel provides heating for cold weather and that the pens are large enough for your dog to move around freely. Ask what exercise facilities they provide. All reputable kennels will be happy to show you around.

If your dog needs to take regular medication or is on a special diet, make sure the kennel staff are aware of this and prepared to follow your instructions. Leave them the name of your vet, just in case.

Another option may be to ask a friend or neighbour to pop in and care for your dog whilst you are away, since most dogs are happier in their familiar surroundings. On the other hand, if your pet is on regular medication requiring your friend to administer tablets, then this may be inconvenient for them. It may be better to leave your dog with an experienced kennel owner than with a novice neighbour.

> **Reputable kennels will be happy to show you around.**

Now your dog has reached the senior stage of their life, several health problems become more likely to occur. Just as you might expect to see your doctor more frequently as you get older, you should make sure your dog visits your vet at least once a year, and preferably more often. After all, taking your dog only once a year for a health check is like you visiting your doctor every five to seven years.

Don't forget that this is about the last chance you will have to obtain health insurance for your dog, since many pet insurance companies will not insure dogs over the age of 8 years. If you do not already have your dog insured, then find out about it soon.

In this section we take a closer look at the routine health care programme for your older dog, plus we give you tips on how to recognise the early warning signs of the common diseases of older dogs.

One of the best friends your dog can have is their vet, so make sure you are registered with a local practice and ask your vet to give your dog a thorough health check at least once a year.

NEUTERING

Generally dogs are neutered as young puppies at around six months old. If for any reason your dog has not been neutered, then discuss this with your vet now. There are a variety of conditions which become more common once pets reach middle age that can be prevented by neutering. These include:

✗ Pyometra (or womb infection). This is a potentially life threatening condition where their womb fills with pus and the dog becomes very ill

✗ Prostate Gland disease. This painful condition is very unusual in neutered dogs

✗ Testicle cancer

✗ Mammary cancer. Research has shown that by spaying your bitch you can dramatically reduce the chance that she will go on to develop mammary cancer

VACCINATIONS

The fact that your dog has reached his older years does not avoid the need for vaccinations. Your dog's immunity may wane as he gets older and so regular booster vaccinations remain essential.

There are several important diseases that can be prevented through routine annual vaccinations. These include:

✗ Distemper

✗ Canine Hepatitis

✗ Leptospirosis

✗ Para influenza

✗ Parvovirus

✗ Rabies (needed if you wish to take your dog abroad)

✗ Kennel cough

As well as giving your dog a boost to his immunity, the annual vaccination is a good chance to let your vet give your dog a comprehensive health check. It is surprising how many times a vet will find the early warning signs of many diseases during a routine booster vaccination. Try to think of the annual health check as an MOT, just like you would have done on your older car.

Remember that good kennels will insist your dog is up to date with his booster vaccinations and some insurance companies will do the same.

FLEA CONTROL

Fleas don't know your dog is a senior citizen. Although your dog is older, he may still become infested with fleas. Highly effective flea preparations are now readily available from your vet. Modern products even contain insect growth regulators, which help break the life cycle of the flea (a bit like birth control for fleas!) and so prevent environmental contamination.

Gone are the days when we have to use unpleasant flea sprays that cause distress to our dogs. New preparations are effective and very easily applied, just part the fur at the base of the neck and apply the contents of the vial to your dog's skin.

Remember, dog fleas don't have to live on dogs. They will just as happily feed on your blood too; so if you're being bitten then get your dog checked as soon as possible. Check your dog's coat for black specks on a regular basis. This is one of the earliest signs of a flea problem.

> **Fleas don't know your dog is a senior citizen.**

WORMING

Puppies can be infected with roundworms from their mother immediately following birth. Roundworms are not as common in older dogs but good internal parasite control is still important because if your dog is a scavenger or has had fleas, then there is still a risk of infestation with tapeworms.

Tapeworms lay eggs which are eaten by an intermediate host (a flea) to continue their development. Your dog then eats the immature tapeworms (larvae) as a result of grooming and swallowing fleas. These larvae will then develop into adult tapeworms in your dogs gut. These in turn lay eggs which are then passed by your dog and are then eaten by the intermediate host thus completing the life-cycle.

Dogs can sometimes be infected with a roundworm called Toxocara. This is potentially very hazardous to humans and may cause blindness. All older dogs should continue to be wormed four times a year with a good quality broad spectrum worming preparation.

Ask your vet for a recommendation.

Dog Fact

Adult tapeworms can reach up to 60cm in length!

BODY CONDITION

Some older dogs will lose weight and may have a reduced ability to absorb and digest food. Switching to a better quality, more easily digestible senior food may be all that is required to prevent your dog becoming thin. Excessive weight gain is a more common problem in older dogs. Partly due to a reduced level of activity, obesity in dogs is a major risk factor for many other health problems and should be avoided.

> "*Obesity in dogs is a major factor for many health problems.*"

Overweight dogs are at a greater risk of developing:

✗ joint disease

✗ diabetes

✗ skin disease

✗ heart disease

✗ respiratory disease

✗ liver disease

✗ bladder disease

Because we see our dogs every day, it can be difficult to spot subtle changes in their body weight. This is another reason why annual health checks by your vet are so important. If you do think your dog might be

overweight then it is better to get your vet to help you plan a weight control programme.

Crash diets are to be avoided, especially in older dogs. It is much safer to aim for a gradual rate of weight loss. Safe effective weight loss can be achieved by feeding specially prepared diets. These foods will contain all the vitamins and minerals your dog needs, without all the calories of supermarket dog food.

A loss of sight or hearing is a common problem in older age. Most dogs cope very well with going deaf but practical tips such as waking your dog with a gentle touch, or making sure your dog knows when you have left, can be helpful. Remember too that deaf dogs will need extra care when you are out for a walk as they may get more easily lost since they will not be able to hear your call. Try using special high pitch dog whistles to help your dog locate you especially when you are out in unfamiliar areas.

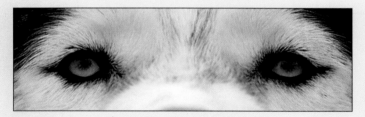

Blindness can be due to cataracts, or more commonly to a condition called sclerosis. This is recognised by a blue-grey haze appearing over your dog's eyes. This is due to age-related changes in the lens. Sclerotic lenses lose their ability to change and quickly alter focus. Affected dogs are less able to see close up objects.

If your dog does go blind, try not to worry, since most dogs cope very well with a loss of sight. Keeping the furniture in the same places at home will allow your dog to remain safe and confident indoors. Remember a blind dog may appear unaffected in familiar surroundings but will need extra attention when away from home.

Dog Fact

Dogs hearing is a lot better than ours. They hear high-pitched sounds that we cannot even detect

Older dogs may lose their sense of taste and smell. This will mean they may become very picky with their food. Try feeding your dog more often with small, frequent meals. This will mean the food will remain fresher and so be more likely to keep its smell. Adding warm water or certain flavourings, such as honey or yeast may also help to stimulate the sense of smell and so improve the appetite.

> ### Dog Fact
>
> In 1925, a Doberman Pinscher named Sauer, tracked a thief 100 miles across the desert in Africa by scent alone

Arthritis is more common in the hip joint in larger breeds.

The surfaces of the joints are normally covered by a smooth layer of protective cartilage and lubricated by special joint fluid. Arthritis occurs in older dogs when, following years of 'wear and tear' this cartilage rubs away and is not efficiently repaired. The result is a rough joint surface which produces inflammation that leads to pain and swelling. It is a very common condition in dogs and may occur following previous joint injury, infection or as a consequence of old age.

Although any joint may be affected, arthritis is more common in the hip joint in larger breed dogs.

The signs of arthritis will depend upon the severity of the changes within the joint and exactly which joints are affected. There are several simple practical steps that you can take to help alleviate the discomfort associated with arthritis.

✓ Control your dog's weight. Simple weight reduction in an overweight dog may be all that is needed to control the signs, since this will dramatically reduce the strain placed on the joints

✓ Massage and groom your dog to improve the circulation and reduce pain from arthritis

✓ Provide a warm supportive bed to helps cushion the joints

✓ Limit the amount of exercise if your dog seems to get stiffer the next day. Many arthritic older dogs will do better with two or three shorter walks each day, rather than one longer hike

If your dog is showing signs of stiffness or lameness ask your vet about the treatments available.

✓ anti-inflammatory tablets or drops

✓ nutrients to protect and repair the cartilage (called chondroprotectives)

✓ injections to help repair the cartilage

✓ hydrotherapy

Dogs of all ages rely on their legs and joints to maintain mobility. Ensuring that your older dog is pain free and still able to benefit from regular exercise is vitally important. Daily exercise is not only essential to keep your dog physically fit, but it will also provide mental stimulation and enjoyment.

The kidneys clean and filter the blood to produce urine. This contains waste products that would be toxic if they built up in your dog's blood.

Kidney disease is very common in older dogs, but can be very difficult to detect. This is because dogs have an amazing ability to control the signs of reduced kidney function until the disease is very advanced. In fact, your dog will only have about a quarter of normal kidney function remaining when your vet is first able to diagnose it.

One of the earliest signs of kidney disease is an increased thirst. You may notice that your dog wakes you at night needing to go out to the toilet, or that he suddenly no longer appears house trained.

Other signs to watch out for include:

✗ poor appetite

✗ vomiting

✗ weight loss

✗ lack of grooming

✗ smelly breath

A blood and urine test will easily diagnose kidney disease and your vet will probably advise a special diet and possibly some tablets to control your dog's blood pressure.

DIABETES

Older dogs are prone to developing diabetes, especially if they are also overweight. Diabetes is a condition where there is excess sugar in the blood. It is caused by a lack of the hormone insulin or obesity.

Diabetes is more common in older female dogs of certain breeds including the Labrador Retriever, Siberian Husky and Keeshond. If your dog develops diabetes you may notice any of the following signs:

✗ extreme thirst (you may not detect your dog has started to drink more but may be aware of increased urination)

✗ weight loss despite a very good appetite

✗ cataracts

If your dog is diagnosed with diabetes your vet may advise a special diet, daily insulin injections or tablets to control the blood sugar level.

Most affected dogs are very bright and alert but if left untreated for some time may start to be sick, become weak and stop eating. You may notice your dog has a sweet 'pear drop' smell on his breath. This is a more serious type of diabetes and you should contact your vet urgently.

HYPOTHYROIDISM

This is a common condition of older dogs, which results in an under production of the thyroid hormone. This condition is seen most commonly in Dobermanns, Golden Retrievers and Boxers.

If you suspect your dog may have an underactive thyroid, then a simple blood test is all that is needed to confirm this. Your vet may then prescribe daily thyroid hormone replacement tablets.

This reduces your dog's metabolic rate and so you may notice:

✗ weight gain

✗ poor skin or excessive hair loss

✗ thirst

✗ a slow heart rate

✗ your dog may appear to be cold or seek out warm places to lie

✗ lethargy

CUSHING'S DISEASE

Older dogs may develop a problem with the adrenal gland leading to an excessive production of cortisol. This is called hyperadrenocorticism, or Cushing's disease.

The treatment for Cushing's Disease will depend on the exact cause of the condition but will usually involve giving your dog some daily medication.

The main signs you may notice are:

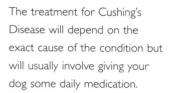

✗ thirst

✗ hunger

✗ panting

✗ weakness

✗ swollen tummy

✗ hair loss and a change in the texture or colour of the skin

Some large breed dogs are prone to a heart muscle disorder called cardiomyopathy. This is more common in certain breeds including the Dobermann, Great Dane, Newfoundland, Golden Retriever, Boxer and Irish Wolfhound.

Dogs can have heart disease that remains undetected for many months, since they are able to reduce their activity level to compensate. You may confuse this with your dog just 'getting older'.

Other signs of heart disease include:

✗ coughing

✗ weight loss

✗ periods of apparent weakness or collapse at rest or during exercise

✗ excessive panting

✗ increased thirst

✗ enlarged tummy due to fluid accumulation

Your vet may be able to detect an abnormal rhythm called a heart murmur during an examination with a stethoscope.

If heart disease is suspected then a variety of extra tests may be indicated. These include:

✓ x-rays

✓ a heart trace (called an electrocardiogram – ECG)

✓ a heart scan (called an ultrasound scan)

✓ blood tests

Modern treatments for heart disease are often very successful and include:

✓ diuretic medication to reduce the accumulation of fluid

✓ medication to help regulate the heart rhythm and prevent abnormal beats

✓ medication to control the blood pressure

Your vet may also recommend a special diet or supplements together with weight control if your dog is overweight. This will also help ease the workload of the heart.

Liver disorders are not as common in older dogs and, because the liver has a multitude of functions and an amazing capacity to repair and regenerate, clinical signs are very varied and therefore less obvious. Common signs of liver disorders in dogs include:

✗ depression or lethargy

✗ weakness

✗ yellow colouration to gums and eyes (called jaundice)

✗ weight loss

✗ thirst

✗ swollen tummy

✗ excessive dribbling

✗ fits

Your vet will need to take a blood test and possibly a biopsy of your dog's liver to confirm the diagnosis. Treatment may involve a special diet, antibiotics and anti-inflammatory drugs but is often very effective.

Older female dogs may start to leak urine, especially when they are relaxed or asleep. This can be due to a weakness of the bladder muscles and may respond to hormone drops in the food. Changes in your dog's mental status may also lead to incontinence. Your dog simply forgets she needs to go.

Urinary incontinence can result in bacterial infection of the bladder, called cystitis. Your vet may advise a special diet or a course of antibiotic tablets.

Older dogs may also develop cystitis due to bladder stones and crystals. These cases will need other treatments including:

✓ a special diet to dissolve stones, or stop crystals forming

✓ surgery to remove bladder stones

✓ antibiotics to treat infections

✓ anti-inflammatory medications

Your dog simply forgets she needs to go.

Cancer is a very common problem in older dogs. Any part of the body may be affected and the symptoms will therefore depend on where the cancer is located. Common types of cancer in older dogs include:

✗ mammary cancer in bitches

✗ skin cancer

✗ cancer of the spleen

✗ bone tumours

✗ lymphoma (cancer of the blood cells)

If you notice any lumps, bumps or swellings appearing on your dog then it is vital to ask your vet to assess them as soon as possible.

Not all growths are cancerous. Lipomas are very common fatty lumps that appear under the skin of older dogs. They are harmless, but may require removal if they are large. If the lump is cancerous then early detection and removal will dramatically improve the success rate.

Other signs of cancer include:

✗ weight loss

✗ diarrhoea

✗ vomiting

✗ pain

✗ poor coat condition

If your vet suspects your dog has cancer then he may suggest:

✓ taking a small piece of the lump and sending it off for microscopic examination (called a biopsy)

✓ surgery to remove the entire lump

✓ chemotherapy (using both tablets and injections)

✓ radiation therapy

✓ a change in diet

Despite our fears of cancer, many dogs respond very well to treatment. Dogs show fewer side effects during chemotherapy than people and often tolerate the drugs very well. Hair loss is unusual.

The key to success is early diagnosis, so don't avoid seeking veterinary attention just because you are worried it could be cancer. Get your dog checked today for peace of mind. Even if there is something wrong, early detection can help.

Your healthy older dog can benefit from a diet that is specially formulated for pets over the age of seven years. Dogs with specific health problems may require special foods that help them cope with the condition. Ask your vet for a recommendation.

HEALTHY SENIOR DOG

The optimal diet for the older dog has:

✓ superior antioxidant formula to help maintain a healthy immune system and delay the signs of premature ageing
✓ a lower level of fat and calories to help maintain ideal bodyweight
✓ omega-3 and omega-6 fatty acids for a healthy skin and coat
✓ low phosphorus and salt to help maintain good kidney function

An ideal food is Hill's* Science Plan* Canine Senior.*

SENIOR DOG PRONE TO WEIGHT GAIN

The optimal diet for the older dog prone to weight gain also has an even lower fat level plus additional L-carnitine to help control weight gain resulting from excess body fat. An ideal food is Hill's* Science Plan* Canine Light Senior.*

DOGS OVER THEIR IDEAL BODYWEIGHT

Overweight senior dogs are at a greater risk of developing many common medical conditions including diabetes, arthritis and heart problems. If your dog is overweight then early dietary intervention is important to help prevent such conditions. Your vet may recommend Hill's* Prescription Diet* Canine r/d.*

DENTAL PROBLEMS

Once your dog's teeth have been professionally cleaned your vet may recommend a change of diet to help maintain oral health. An ideal food is Hill's* Prescription Diet* Canine t/d*. This food acts like an edible toothbrush and helps wipe plaque from the surface of the teeth with every bite.

BRAIN AGEING

If your dog is showing signs of premature brain ageing (which include disturbed sleep, reduced interaction, loss of house training) your vet may recommend a food supplemented with high levels of nutritional antioxidants which reduce oxidative damage to the brain cells.
An ideal food is Hill's* Prescription Diet* Canine b/d.*

KIDNEY PROBLEMS

If your dog has kidney problems look for a product that provides:

✓ a controlled protein level

✓ low phosphorus and salt levels

Your vet may recommend Hill's* Prescription Diet* Canine k/d.*

DIABETES

Your vet may recommend a high fibre, controlled energy food such as Hill's* Prescription Diet* Canine w/d*. Avoid soft moist 'morsel' type dog foods since these foods tend to be high in sugars.

Heart Problems

Your vet may recommend a change of diet if your dog develops a heart problem. Exactly which diet is chosen will depend upon the type of heart condition your dog has.

Bladder Problems

If your dog forms crystals in his urine your vet may recommend a special food to help reduce the risk of these forming. Exactly which type of diet is recommended will depend upon the type of crystals your dog has produced.

Cancer

If your dog is diagnosed with cancer your vet may recommend Hill's* Prescription Diet* Canine n/d*. This special food has been proven in clinical trials to improve the quality of life for dogs undergoing chemotherapy or radiation treatment for cancer.

Water

Your dog must have an adequate supply of fresh water at all times. Not having water to drink for a sustained length of time can harm your dog's health.

You can't stop your dog getting older. But regular check ups from your vet, a good diet and a routine health care programme will go a long way to ensuring your dog continues to live a long and healthy life. Remember, you know your dog better than anyone else and so your observations will be vitally important in guiding your vet towards any changes that have started to occur.

And just remember "there's only one best dog in the world…and everybody owns him!"